OVERSIZE

G. Poggenpohl

Cooking Wild Game

Thirty-Six Hearty Dishes

Schiffer Publishing Ltd®

4880 Lower Valley Road   Atglen, Pennsylvania 19310

Other Schiffer Books By The Author:
Cooking Together: Having Fun with Two or More Cooks in the Kitchen, 978-0-7643-3647-8, $19.99
Cooking with Mustard: Empowering your Palate, 978-0-7643-3643-0, $19.99

Other Schiffer Books on Related Subjects:
Today I Cook: A Man's Guide to the Kitchen, 978-0-7643-3644-7, $19.99
Creative Ideas for Garnishing & Decorating, 978-0-7643-3645-4, $19.99
Asparagus & Strawberries, 978-0-7643-3648-5, $19.99

Translated from the German by Dr. Edward Force
Photos: Food in Wort und Bild, Sigmarszell
Kitchen: Corinna Brunner
Layout: Baerbel Bach

Type set in Zurich Lt.

ISBN: 978-0-7643-3646-1
Printed in China

Schiffer Books are available at special discounts for bulk purchases for sales promotions or premiums. Special editions, including personalized covers, corporate imprints, and excerpts can be created in large quantities for special needs. For more information contact the publisher:

Published by Schiffer Publishing Ltd.
4880 Lower Valley Road
Atglen, PA 19310
Phone: (610) 593-1777; Fax: (610) 593-2002
E-mail: Info@schifferbooks.com

For the largest selection of fine reference books on this and related subjects, please visit our web site at
www.schifferbooks.com
We are always looking for people to write books on new and related subjects. If you have an idea for a book please contact us at the above address.

This book may be purchased from the publisher.
Include $5.00 for shipping.
Please try your bookstore first.
You may write for a free catalog.

In Europe, Schiffer books are distributed by
Bushwood Books
6 Marksbury Ave.
Kew Gardens
Surrey TW9 4JF England
Phone: 44 (0) 20 8392 8585; Fax: 44 (0) 20 8392 9876
E-mail: info@bushwoodbooks.co.uk
Website: www.bushwoodbooks.co.uk

G. Poggenpohl

Cooking Wild Game

Thirty-Six Hearty Dishes

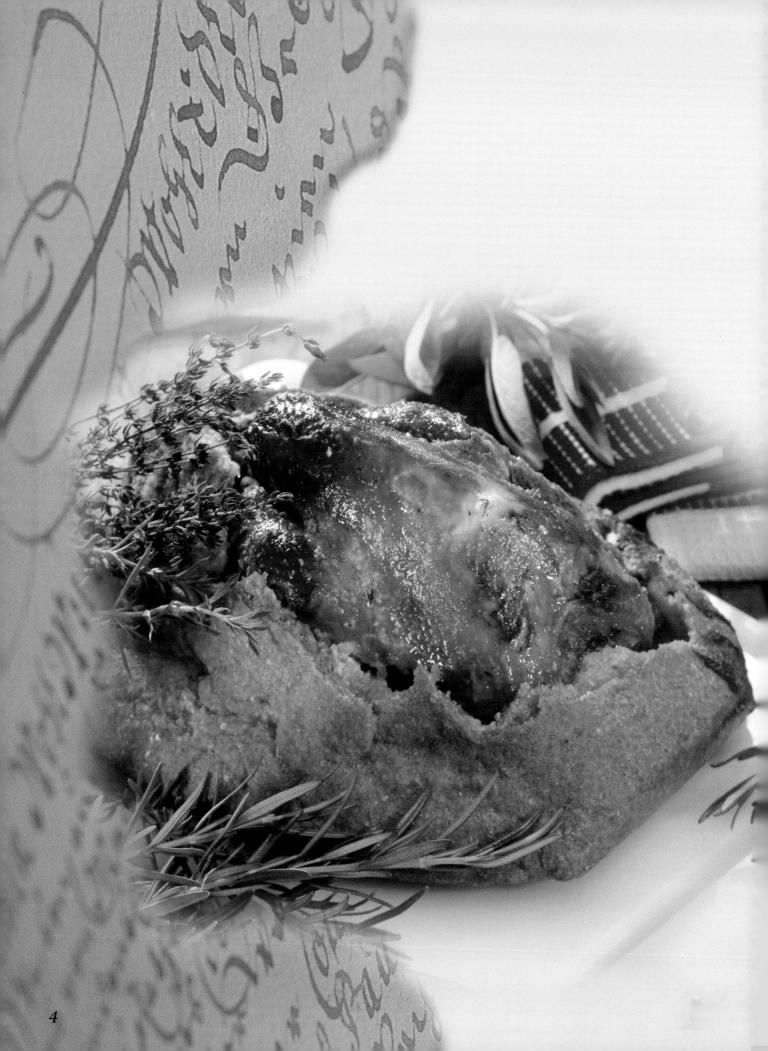

4

Foreword

Many thousands of years ago, wild meats were part of mankind's natural food diet.

Later, man discovered animal husbandry and domesticated wild animals, which were nourished with their natural foods. In the present day, the day of commercial farming, man deliberately influences the taste of meat. This book offers you the opportunity to experience the original taste of meat, the chance to taste many kinds of wild meat.

A juicy wild boar roast, for example, offers you this taste experience.

Sample wild fowls that have grown up in their natural environment and have an intense flavor. Unlike the farm-raised, farm-fed animals, wild meat is very low in fat.

The recipes included in this book show you how to prepare wild meat in many variations with many flavor profiles. You will find new but tested recipes from venison to rabbit to guinea fowl.

If you want to offer your guests something special, serve them a wild meat dish!

Yours,
G. Poggenpohl

Advice

In choosing a way to prepare wild meats, the age of the animal plays a decisive role. Older animals, such as deer, chamois, or hare, can become softer and more wholesome by first soaking in a marinade for two to three days. The same also applies to game birds. The marinade should always be carefully measured so that the meat to be treated is completely covered. Also, marinating meat must always be refrigerated. For wild game marinades use root vegetables, like carrots, celery, leeks, onions, and parsley roots. Suitable spices include peppercorns, juniper berries, laurel leaves, thyme, cloves, coriander, and pimento. Other spices can also be used to infuse the meat with flavor. Try rosemary, sage, ginger, and garlic.

After soaking in the marinade, you can use the meat or bird as described in the recipes. **All recipes serve four people.**

The following marinades are especially suitable:

Wine Marinade

Cook vinegar and water in equal parts with root vegetables and herbs and let cool. After cooling, add the same amount of white or red wine and immerse the meat in it.

Vinegar Marinade

Cook vinegar and water in equal parts with root vegetables and herbs, let cool, and then immerse the meat in it. Since vinegar changes the flavor of the meat, you should use high-quality wine vinegar.

Buttermilk or Sour Milk Marinade

Mix buttermilk or sour milk with root vegetables and herbs and immerse the meat in it.

Measurements

Both metric and standard equivalents are used in these recipes. As a reference, here is a list of abbreviations used for the metric quantities and some common metric conversions.

kg kilogram
g gram
ml milliliter
1l 1 liter = 1000 ml = 1 kg = 1000 g

Roe Venison Saddle en Papillote

Ingredients

3 1/3 lb (1 1/2kg) roe venison saddle
3/4 cup (100g) American sunflower seeds
4 slices toasted wheat bread
3 1/2 tablespoons (50g) soft butter
2 egg yolks
20 juniper berries
5 pimento peppercorns
2 tablespoons cut rosemary leaves
1 teaspoon Dijon mustard
salt, pepper
1/2 pound (250g) seedless grapes
parchment paper

Preparation

1. Remove skin and tendons from the venison saddle and cut 3/4 inch (2cm) deep on each side of the bone.

2. Cut up the sunflower seeds coarsely, toast the bread and crumble until fine. Work the crumbs into a mixture with the sunflower seeds, butter, egg yolks, crushed juniper berries, pimento peppercorns, rosemary leaves, mustard, salt, and pepper.

3. Preheat the oven to 400°F (200°C).

4. Lay out two pieces of parchment paper large enough to cover the venison and grease with butter. Place the venison on the parchment paper and brush on the sunflower seed mixture, filling in the cuts you made along the bone.

5. Wash the grapes, remove from the stems, and lay them around the venison.

6. Fold the parchment paper loosely over the meat and close the edges firmly. Put the package in a roasting pan and roast for fifty minutes on the middle shelf. Then open the paper at the top. Roast another ten minutes. Let the venison roast stand for at least five minutes.

7. Loosen the fillets from the bones and cut into slices. Plate with grapes and juice from the pan.

Tip: catch the meat drippings, cook with game broth, and thin with cold butter or crème fraîche.

Roe Venison

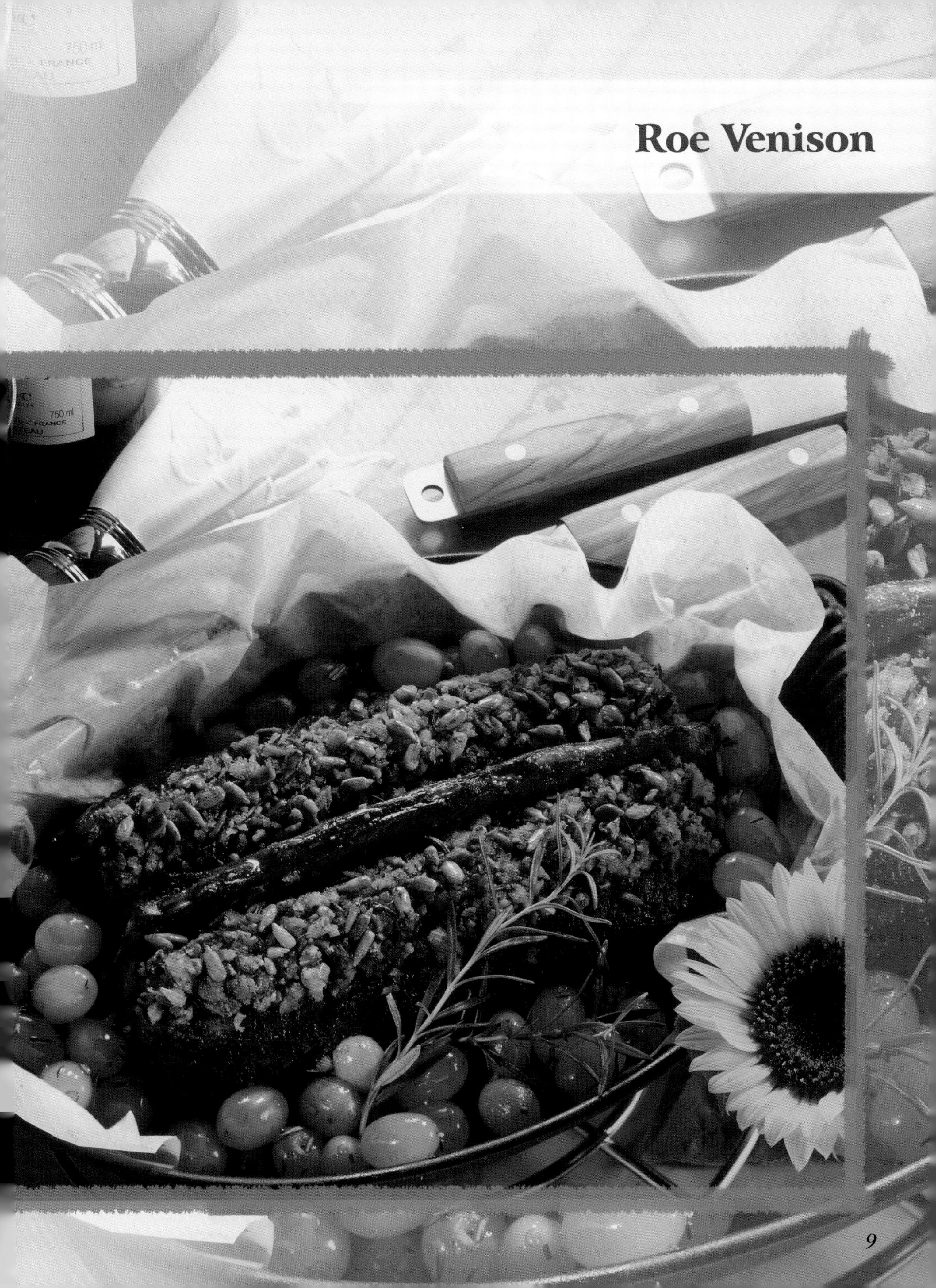

Roe Venison Loin with Almond Crust

Ingredients

1 1/3 lb (600g) roe venison loin

For the sauce
1 3/4 lb (800g) venison bones, cut small
1 2/3 cups (400ml) game broth
1 cup (1/4l) red wine, 1/2 cup (1/8l) port wine
2 tablespoons balsamic vinegar
1 teaspoon sugar
1 onion
1 carrot
1 small piece celery in cubes
1 tablespoon cold butter
salt and pepper

For the almond crust
7 tablespoons (100g) butter
1/3 cup (30g) ground California almonds
1 1/8 cup (40g) roughly grated white bread
1/4 cup (20g) California almond slices
salt, pepper

For the polenta
1 cup (250ml) milk
1 cup (250 ml) water
1/2 cup (80g) polenta
4 1/4 cups (300g) broccoli
salt
nutmeg
butter

Preparation

1. Brown the venison loin on high heat all around. Salt and pepper it. Then roast it for about twenty-five minutes at 250°F (130°C) in a preheated oven.

2. Whisk the butter to a foam for the almond crust, add salt and pepper. Mix in the ground almonds and the almond slices and put aside.

3. Caramelize the sugar for the sauce. Add the deer bones and vegetables, brown them, and pour in red wine, port wine, and balsamic vinegar. Let it reduce. Then fill it up with game broth and cook the broth down half way. Strain the sauce, bring it to a boil, and stir in the cold butter. Season to taste with salt and pepper and remove it from the stove.

4. For the polenta, heat the milk and water with salt, add the polenta, and let it cook a few minutes, stirring it. Transfer the mixture to a baking sheet sprinkled with water and let it cool. Cut out small half-moons with a small cookie cutter and fry them in butter.

5. Cook the broccoli in salt water. Then toss it in butter and flavor with nutmeg.

6. Brush the almond crust onto the venison loins and broil until the crust is light brown. Plate the venison, broccoli, and polenta, add the sauce then serve.

Roe Venison Thigh with Mustard and Thyme Sauce

Ingredients

2 1/4 lbs (1kg) roe venison thigh, deep-frozen
salt, pepper
4 tablespoons cooking oil
1 1/2 cups (375ml) meat broth
1/2 cup (125ml) dry white wine
1-2 tablespoons medium hot mustard
1 tablespoon Bavarian sweet mustard
1 tablespoon crème fraîche
2 tablespoons thyme
1 tablespoon dark gravy mix

Preparation

1. Defrost the venison thigh and season with salt and pepper. Heat oil in a pot and brown all sides of the thigh. Pour in the broth and stew for about seventy minutes on low heat.

2. Take out the meat and keep it warm. Pour on the game broth with the wine. Season with mustard, crème fraîche, and thyme. Let it cook and thicken with the gravy mix.

3. Cut the venison thigh into slices and plate it with the sauce.

4. Serve with noodles and red beet salad. Add a fresh thyme sprig for garnish.

Tip: Use fresh thyme in your preparation.

Roe Venison Fillet Hubertus

Ingredients

1 1/3 lbs (600g) roe venison fillet
2 tablespoons frying fat
3/8 cup (100ml) red wine
3 1/3 cups (200g) chanterelle mushrooms
2 tablespoons crème fraîche
1 tablespoon cornstarch
4 pears
2 tablespoons butter
salt and pepper

Preparation

1. Remove the skin and tendons from the venison fillet and season the meat with salt and pepper.

2. Heat the frying fat in a pan and fry the fillet on both sides for a total of fifteen minutes. Wrap the fillet in aluminum foil and let it stand for about fifteen minutes.

3. Mix the red wine with a tablespoon of cornstarch and simmer it with the drippings from the fillet pan, season with salt and pepper.

4. Heat a tablespoon of butter and fry the mushrooms. Stir in the crème fraîche, season with salt and pepper.

5. Cut the pears into wedges and remove the cores. Melt a tablespoon of butter in a pan and simmer the pears in it.

6. Take the fillet out of the foil, cut it up, and plate it with the pears and the chanterelle mushrooms.

Fallow Venison Medallions in Pepper Sauce

Ingredients

1 1/4 cups (200g) Camargue rice (or wild rice)
1 3/4 lbs (800g) fallow venison medallions
3 tablespoons cooking oil
2 soft pears
1 cup (1/4l) game broth
1 1/3 tablespoons (2cl) Madeira
1 glass sweet cream
2 tablespoons peppercorns
salt
2 2/3 cups (200g) oyster mushrooms

Preparation

1. Cook the rice as instructed on the package.

2. Let the venison medallions defrost, heat two tablespoons oil in a pan and fry the medallions about two minutes on each side, keep them warm.

3. Quarter the pears, remove the core, peel, cube, and cook briefly in frying fat. Pour in the game broth and the Madeira, let it cook, and then puree the mixture. Add the cream and the peppercorns and let the sauce reduce.

4. Clean the oyster mushrooms, wash, dice, and fry in the remaining oil. Mix into the rice.

5. Plate the medallions and ladle on the sauce. Serve with the rice on the side.

Fallow Venison

Venison Steaks with Cheese and Herb Crust

Ingredients

4 fallow venison steaks
4 slices of toasted bread
3/4 cup (100g) crumbled blue cheese
1/2 bunch thyme
2 tablespoons frying fat
salt and pepper

Preparation

1. Preheat the oven to 400°F (200°C).

2. Tear the toast into pieces, add thyme leaves and blue cheese, and mix in a blender.

3. Season the venison steaks with salt and pepper. Heat the frying fat in a pan and fry the steaks on both sides for about four minutes.

4. Put the steaks in a baking pan and spoon the cheese crust on top. Bake for about ten minutes.

5. Serve the steaks with mixed vegetables.

Venison in Fruit Sauce

Ingredients

1 lb (400g) fallow venison cubes
2 tablespoons sunflower oil
2 shallots
1 cup (200ml) game broth
3 1/3 tablespoons (50ml) orange juice
4 tablespoons mango chutney
1 tablespoon light gravy mix
1 papaya
salt and pepper

Preparation

1. Defrost the venison and season with salt and pepper. Heat the oil in a pot and brown the meat. Take the meat out of the pan and keep it warm.

2. Peel the shallots, dice, and simmer in the venison drippings. Pour in the game broth and orange juice, add the mango chutney, and let it simmer for a little bit. Thicken with light gravy mix.

3. Peel the papaya, remove the seeds with a knife, cube, and add to the sauce with the venison.

4. Plate the venison and serve with thin green noodles and exotic fruits.

Bohemian Venison Roulade

Ingredients

1-2 small onions (50g)
3-4 shallots (50g)
3/4 cup (50g) champignon mushrooms
2 French carrots (50g)
2 stalks celery (50g)
4 thin fallow venison cutlets
4 very thin slices bacon
4 dried plums
4 dried apricots

4 walnuts
1/8 cup (50g) clarified butter
1 laurel leaf
5 juniper berries
1 2/3 cups (400ml) game broth
1 cup (1/4l) red wine
1/2 cup (100g) sweet cream
salt and pepper

Preparation

1. Peel the onions and shallots, cut the onions into rings, quarter the shallots. Clean the mushrooms and cut into thin slices. Clean the carrots and celery, wash, peel, and dice.

2. Season the venison roulades with salt and pepper. Cover each cutlet with a strip of bacon, a few mushrooms, thin onion rings, one plum, apricot and walnut each, and roll up tightly. Tie them together with kitchen string.

3. Heat the clarified butter in a pot. Fry the roulades. Fry the vegetables and shallots briefly along with them. Add the laurel leaf and juniper berries and moisten with the game broth and red wine. Add salt and pepper. Let them stew covered for about 40 minutes.

4. Then take out the roulades, pour the broth through a sieve, add cream, and lightly simmer. Serve the roulades with the sauce.

Steamed pears with cranberries and potato slices are tasty accompaniments to this dish.

Chamois Roast in Juniper Gravy

Ingredients

2 1/4 lb (1kg) chamois roast
1 carrot
2 onions
1 tablespoon juniper berries
1 tablespoon pepper corns
1 clove
2 laurel leaves
1/2 cup (1/8l) vinegar
1/2 cup (1/8l) red wine
3 3/4 cups (250g) mushrooms
1 cup crème fraîche
1 teaspoon sugar
frying fat
salt and pepper

Preparation

1. Peel the onions and carrot and cut into pieces. Mash the peppercorns and juniper berries in a mortar. Pour the vinegar and red wine into a bowl, add the vegetables, laurel leaves, clove, peppercorns, and juniper berries. Place the chamois roast in the marinade and put in the refrigerator covered for about two days. Turn the meat several times while marinating.

2. Take the meat out of the marinade, dry, and season with salt and pepper. Strain the marinade and put it aside.

3. Preheat the oven to 400°F (200°C). Heat the frying fat in a large casserole dish or a Dutch oven and brown the roast on all sides in it. Pour on half the marinade, cover, and place in the oven to stew for about 60 minutes. Occasionally pour the remaining marinade over the roast.

4. Clean the mushrooms and cut into slices. Crush the rest of the juniper berries in a mortar or grind them.

5. Take the roast out of the pot and keep it warm. Stir the mushrooms, crème fraîche, and juniper berries into the sauce, season to taste with salt, pepper, and sugar.

6. Carve the roast and serve with the sauce.

Chamois Fillet with Sour Cherry Sauce

Ingredients

1 1/3 lb (600g) chamois fillet
2 cups (500g) sour cherries
1 cup (1/4l) red wine
1/4 cup (50g) sugar
1 cinnamon stick
4 cloves
1/8 cup (20g) grated ginger
several sage leaves
1 tablespoon cornstarch
2 tablespoons olive oil
salt and pepper

Preparation

1. Pour out the sour cherries, keep the juice, and cut the cherries into pieces. Peel the ginger and grate fine.

2. Remove skin and tendons from the chamois fillet and season with salt and pepper. Heat the olive oil in a pan and fry the fillet on all sides, 15 minutes total. Wrap the fillet in aluminum foil and let it stand.

3. Stir the red wine and cornstarch together. Pour the red wine into the frying fat, add the sour cherries, ginger, herbs, and sage leaves. Simmer and flavor with sugar, salt, and pepper. If the sauce gets too thick, thin it with some cherry juice.

4. Take the chamois fillet out of the foil, cut it up, and serve with the cherry sauce.

Wild Boar Ragout Savoy

Ingredients

1 1/3 lb (600g) wild boar meat
2 tablespoons olive oil
3 cloves garlic
2 cups (1/2l) white wine
5-6 shallots (100g)
1 1/2 cups (100g) mushrooms
1-2 tomatoes (100g)
1 bunch mixed herbs
1 tablespoon flour
salt and pepper

Preparation

1. Cut the wild boar meat into 3/4 inch (2cm) pieces. Heat the frying fat in a pot and fry the meat on high heat. Mix in the flour and fry for about one minute, then pour in the white wine and simmer about 20 minutes

2. Peel the garlic cloves and shallots. Quarter the shallots and slice the garlic. Clean the mushrooms, wash the tomatoes, and cut into bite-size chunks. Steam the herbs, pick the leaves from the stems, and cut up coarsely.

3. Add the vegetables and herbs to the meat and let them cook for about three or four minutes. Season the ragout to taste with salt and pepper and serve.

Wild Boar Roast in Fruit Sauce

Ingredients

2 1/4 lb (1kg) wild boar roast
2 tablespoons frying fat
2/3 lb (300g) black currants
1 cup (1/4l) meat broth
1/4 cup (50g) sugar
salt and pepper

Preparation

1. Pick and wash the currants.

2. Season the wild boar roast with salt and pepper. Heat the frying fat in a large casserole dish or Dutch oven and brown the roast on all sides. Add half the broth and 2/3 of the currants.

3. Put the roast in an oven preheated to 400°F (200°C) and roast for about an hour and a half. Baste the roast frequently, adding more meat broth if necessary.

4. Take the roast out of the pot and keep it warm.

5. Stir the rest of the broth and the sugar into the sauce and puree it. Add the rest of the currants to the sauce, let them simmer briefly, and season to taste with salt and pepper.

6. Carve the roast and plate with the sauce. Dumplings go nicely with this dish.

Wild Boar Goulash with Dark Beer

Ingredients

1 1/2 lb (700g) wild boar cubes
3-4 large onions (500g)
2 garlic cloves
1 lemon
4 tablespoons mild paprika powder
1 tablespoon hot paprika powder
1 tablespoon mustard
1 tablespoon marjoram
1/2 teaspoon cumin
4 1/4 cups (1l) malt beer
salt and pepper

Preparation

1. Peel the onions and garlic, then dice. Wash and dry the marjoram and pick the leaves from the stems.

2. Heat the frying fat in a pot, add the onions, and brown them. Add the wild boar cubes to the onions and brown on high heat. Sprinkle in the paprika powder and add the beer.

3. Stir in the garlic, marjoram, cumin, and mustard. Mix everything and simmer on low heat covered for about forty minutes. The goulash is finished when it is dark and gleaming. Season to taste with salt and pepper and serve.

Wild Boar Roast with Honey Crust

Ingredients

2 1/4 lb (1kg) wild boar roast
2/3 cup (150ml) honey
1 cup (250ml) malt beer
2 3/4 tablespoons (4cl) brandy
1 lemon
1 tablespoon mild paprika powder
7 tablespoons (100g) butter
1 glass sweet cream
salt and pepper

Preparation

1. Preheat the oven to 350°F (180°C). Squeeze the lemon.

2. Make a marinade with the honey, malt beer, brandy, lemon juice, and paprika powder.

3. Season the wild boar roast with salt and pepper. Heat the butter in a large casserole dish or Dutch oven and brown the roast.

4. Brush the marinade over the boar and roast in the oven for about an hour and a half. Brush the roast frequently until there is no marinade left.

5. Take the roast out of the dish and keep it warm. Pour the cream in with the drippings and the remaining sauce and reduce it. If the sauce should become too thin, let it simmer a little longer, then season to taste with salt and pepper.

6. Carve the roast and plate with the sauce.

Hare Roulades Argentine

Ingredients

1 1/3 lb (600g) hare saddle fillets
salt and pepper
2 tablespoons crème fraîche
8 slices raw smoked bacon
1 small onion
2 shallots
1 French carrot

1 apple
2 tablespoons cooking oil
3 tablespoons Calvados
1 cup (250ml) vegetable broth
3 leaves lemon mint
2 clove buds
2 tablespoon cider

Preparation

1. Defrost the hare fillets as instructed on the package, wash, pat dry, halve lengthwise, and beat into long thin roulade strips.

2. Season with salt and pepper, brush with crème fraîche, and put a slice of bacon on each.

3. Peel the onion and the shallots and dice. Wash and peel the carrot and the apple. Halve the apple, remove the core, and dice. Sprinkle the onion and apple cubes on the bacon slices. Roll up the fillet strips and tie with kitchen string. Brown the rolls on all sides in heated oil.

4. Add the carrot, shallot, and remaining apple cubes to the roulades and simmer. Pour in the Calvados and the vegetable broth. Add the cloves and cook about twenty minutes over medium heat.

5. Take out the roulades and keep them warm. Remove the cloves and puree the drippings. Season to taste with the cider, salt, and pepper.

6. Fry the remaining bacon until crisp and wrap it around the hare roulades. Plates and serve with potatoes au gratin.

Hare Pot Pie Lucullus

Ingredients

1 lb (400g) hare meat
2 tablespoons frying fat
2 packages puff pastry
4 spring onions
2 French carrots
Fat to grease the baking form or pie pan
1 egg yolk to brush on
salt and pepper

Preparation

1. Cut the hare meat into small pieces and season with salt and pepper. Heat the frying fat in a pan and brown the meat for seven minutes.

2. Let the dough defrost.

3. Clean and wash the spring onions and peel and wash the carrots. Cut the onions into rings and the carrots into thin slices.

4. Grease a baking form or pie pan and line the pan with one of the puff pastries, making the edges high. Pour in the rabbit meat and distribute the vegetables.

5. Form a top crust of the remaining dough, laying it over the filling. Press the edge down firmly and perforate several times with a fork. Beat the egg yolk and brush it on the dough.

6. Bake it for about twenty-five minutes or until golden brown in an oven preheated to 400°F (200°C). Serve garnished with fresh herbs.

Hare in Juniper Cream Sauce

Ingredients

2 hare saddles (each about 1 1/3 lb [600g])
salt and pepper
1 tablespoon juniper berries
2-3 medium onions (250g)
1-2 potatoes (150g)
2 French carrots
1 parsley root
1 tablespoon clarified butter
2 cups (1/2l) game broth
1/4 lb (100g) breakfast bacon in thin slices
1 cup (250g) sweet cream

For the Hazel Nut Brussels Sprouts

1 1/2 lbs (700g) Brussels sprouts
3 tablespoons hazel nut slices
1 tablespoon clarified butter
1 glass game broth
salt and nutmeg

Preparation

1. Rub the hare saddles with salt, pepper, and crushed juniper berries. Put them in the refrigerator covered for several hours.

2. Peel and dice the onions, potatoes, carrots, and parsley root.

3. Heat the butter in a large frying pan and brown the hare meat. Then add the cubed vegetables, fry briefly and pour in the game broth. Put slices of bacon on the hare meat and stew covered for twenty to thirty minutes at 425°F (225°C) in a preheated oven.

4. Meanwhile, clean and wash the Brussels sprouts, warm in the clarified butter, and add the game broth. Season with salt and nutmeg. Cook covered for about fifteen minutes.

5. Remove the hare from the oven and wrap it in aluminum foil to keep warm. Meanwhile, puree the drippings with the vegetables, stir in cream, cook thoroughly, and season to taste.

6. Briefly cook the hazel nut slices in a pan without fat and sprinkle on the Brussels sprouts. Unwrap the hare meat and plate with the sauce and Brussels sprouts.

Noodles or potato pancakes go well with these dishes.

Hare Saddle with Chestnut Crust

Ingredients

2 hare saddles (1 1/3 lb [600g], ready to cook)
4 1/4 oz (120g) chestnuts from a can
1 bunch parsley
2 eggs
8 3/4 tablespoons (125g) garlic butter
3/4 cup (45g) hard roll crumbs
salt and pepper

For the sauce

3 tablespoons flour
7/8 cup (200ml) game broth
1 cup (250ml) elderberry juice
3 clove buds
sugar

Preparation

1. Chop the chestnuts finely. Wash the parsley, shake it dry, and chop finely. Whip about four tablespoons (60g) garlic butter with a hand mixer. Add the eggs and mix with the roll crumbs, chestnuts, and parsley. Then salt and pepper the mixture.

2. Cut about 1 1/8 inches (3cm) into the hare saddles along each side of the backbone. Salt and pepper the meat thoroughly. Smear part of the chestnut butter mixture into the cuts. Press the meat down and smear the rest of the mixture on the meat.

3. Grease a baking sheet with about 1 1/3 tablespoons (20g) garlic butter, knead the rest of the butter into the flour and put it in a cold place. Lay the meat on the baking sheet and roast about twelve to fifteen minutes in an oven preheated to 425°F (220 °C).

4. Then turn on the broiler for about three minutes. Turn off the oven and let the meat set until the sauce is finished.

5. Simmer the game broth, elderberry juice, and cloves uncovered for about five minutes. Take the cloves out of the sauce and gradually stir in the flour and garlic butter. Season the sauce to taste with sugar, salt, and pepper. Simmer it lightly. Carefully remove the hare meat from the bones and carve the meat. Serve it with the elderberry sauce.

Rabbit Saddle with Applesauce

Ingredients

1/3 cup (40g) American sunflower seeds
2 large, firm cooking apples
juice of one lemon
2 onions
3 1/2 tablespoons (50g) butter
1/2 teaspoon salt
2 tablespoons maple syrup

1/2 teaspoon sweet-sour ginger
1 shot dry white wine
7/8 cup (200ml) sweet cream
7/8 cup (200ml) veal broth
4 rabbit saddles
2 tablespoons sunflower oil

Preparation

1. Preheat the oven to 425°F (225°C). Roast the sunflower seeds. Wash and peel the apples, remove the cores, and dice. Immediately put them in lemon water so they do not turn brown.

2. Dice the onions and cook them in the butter.

3. Strain the apple cubes and add them to the onions along with the salt, maple syrup, and chopped ginger. Simmer for two minutes, then douse with white wine and cook on low heat. Add the cream and half of the veal broth.

4. Wash the rabbit saddles, pat dry, and brown in heated sunflower oil. Cook for thirty minutes on the middle rack of the oven, baste frequently with the remaining veal broth. When finished, wrap the rabbit meat first in aluminum foil and then in a kitchen towel.

5. Add the sunflower seeds to the pan drippings and sauce and heat. Unwrap the meat, slice it diagonally and serve it with the sauce.

Rice goes best with this dish.

Rabbit Stew

Ingredients

3 1/2 tablespoons (50g) butter
1/8 lb (70g) smoked bacon
1 rabbit (3 1/3-4 1/2 lbs [1 1/2-2kg]) cut
into 8 pieces by butcher
4 tablespoons flour
5-6 small onions (400g)
2 garlic cloves
1 bunch spring onions
4 cups (1l) red wine
3 slices whole-grain rye bread
2-3 laurel leaves
4 clove bulbs
1 glass sweet cream
salt and pepper

Preparation

1. Dice the bacon and render in a large casserole dish or a Dutch oven. Remove the bacon with a ladle and put aside.

2. Peel and halve or quarter the onions. Clean the spring onions and cut into crude pieces. Peel and crush the garlic cloves.

3. Roll the pieces of rabbit in flour and fry in the bacon fat. Add butter.

4. Add the vegetables to the rabbit, pour in red wine, and cook. Add the bread, spices, salt, and pepper.

5. Cover the pot and stew it all in an oven preheated to 400°F (200°C) for sixty to seventy-five minutes.

6. Take the rabbit meat out of the pot and strain the sauce into a medium sauce pan. Heat the sauce again, stir in the cream, and season with salt and pepper. Put the meat, vegetables, and sauce together in a serving dish.

Stewed Rabbit Thighs

Ingredients

3-4 small potatoes (600g)
2 leek stalks
4 stalks celery
4 rabbit thighs
2 tablespoons frying fat
pepper
3 garlic cloves
1 bunch thyme
2 tablespoons fennel seeds

1 tablespoon cardamom seeds
1 laurel leaf
1/2 cup (1/8l) white wine
4 cups (1l) water or vegetable broth
1/2 cup (1/8l) soy sauce
2 tablespoons honey
2/3 cup (100g) dried apricots
salt

Preparation

1. Peel the potatoes, thoroughly clean the leeks and celery, and cut into slices or rings 3/8 inch (1cm) wide.

2. Pepper the rabbit thighs and brown in a large casserole dish or Dutch oven.

3. Add the garlic, thyme, fennel, cardamom, and laurel leaf. Pour in the white wine and cook. Add the broth, soy sauce, and honey, then place in an oven preheated to 400°F (200°C). After thirty minutes, add the potatoes, leeks, celery, and apricots. Stew for thirty more minutes.

4. Take out the rabbit thighs and season the sauce with salt and pepper.

Duck with Apple Calvados Sauce

Ingredients

2 wild ducks
4 apples
2 3/4 tablespoons (4cl) Calvados
1 cup (1/4l) chicken broth
1 glass sweet cream
2 tablespoons frying fat
salt and pepper

Preparation

1. Prepare the wild ducks for roasting. Remove remaining feathers with tweezers and season the ducks with salt and pepper inside and out. Then put them in a large casserole dish or Dutch oven, add the frying fat, and bake for about forty minutes in an oven preheated to 350°F (180°C). Baste the ducks with frying fat occasionally.

2. Wash the apples, quarter, remove the cores, and dice. Just before removing the ducks put half the apple cubes in and let them cook briefly.

3. Take the ducks out of the oven, cut them up, and keep warm.

4. Pour the chicken broth into the duck vessel to deglaze the pan. Add the cream and puree. Stir in the rest of the apples and the Calvados, season with salt and pepper.

5. Dollop apple sauce on serving plates, plate the wild duck pieces on top, and serve.

Tip: With young ducks it is almost impossible to remove all of the pin feathers. A propane torch is helpful for singeing these off.

Wild Duck

51

Wild Duck with Honey Sauce

Ingredients

2 wild ducks
3 tablespoons frying fat
4 3/4 tablespoons (100g) wild honey
1 bunch thyme
1/8 cup (20g) ginger
1 tablespoon lemon juice
3 tablespoons soy sauce
pepper

Preparation

1. Prepare the wild ducks for roasting. Remove remaining feathers with tweezers. Do not spice the wild ducks for this recipe.

2. Wash the thyme, shake it, and pick the leaves from the stems. Peel the ginger and grate it fine. Make a marinade of the honey, ginger, lemon juice, soy sauce, and pepper.

3. Brush the ducks repeatedly with the marinade for several hours and let it dry. Repeat until all the marinade is used.

4. Put the ducks in a large casserole dish or Dutch oven, add the frying fat, and bake for about forty minutes in an oven preheated to 350°F (180°C). Baste the ducks with frying fat occasionally.

5. Take the ducks out of the oven and serve.

Roast Wild Duck on Squash

Ingredients

2 wild ducks
2 tablespoons frying fat
1 bunch mixed herbs
1 1/4 lb (500g) squash or pumpkin
2 tablespoons butter
2 tablespoons sugar
nutmeg
salt and pepper

Preparation

1. Prepare the wild ducks for roasting, removing remaining feathers with tweezers. Season the ducks with salt and pepper inside and outside. Wash the herbs, shake dry, and stuff into the ducks.

2. Put the ducks in a large casserole dish or Dutch oven, brush the frying fat on the ducks, and roast them for about forty minutes in an oven preheated to 350°F (180°C). Baste the ducks with frying fat occasionally.

3. Cut up the squash or pumpkin, remove the seeds, cut off the rind with a knife, and shred the pulp.

4. Ten minutes before the ducks are finished, melt the butter in a pot, add the squash and cook for about five minutes on low heat. Season with sugar, nutmeg, salt, and pepper. Plate the squash.

5. Carve the ducks, place the meat on the squash, and serve.

Salt-Encrusted Pheasant

Ingredients

1 pheasant
1 bunch mixed herbs
2 garlic cloves
8 1/4 cups (2kg) salt
3/4 cup (80g) flour
1/2 cup (80g) cornstarch
1 cup (200g) egg whites

Preparation

1. Wash the pheasant and pat dry. Rinse the herbs, shake them, and stuff them and the garlic into the pheasant.

2. Beat the egg white stiff and mix into a dough with the salt and flour.

3. Line a baking sheet with parchment paper. Pour one third of the dough on the paper so that the entire bottom side of the pheasant would be covered. Set the pheasant on the dough and completely enclose it with the rest of the dough.

4. Bake the pheasant in an oven preheated to 350°F (180°C) for about an hour and a half.

5. Take the pheasant out of the oven, let it stand for 5 to 10 minutes, then break the salt crust with a hammer and carve the pheasant.

Pheasant Breast Salad

Ingredients

2/3 lb (300g) pheasant breast
a variety of salad lettuces
2 shallots
3/4 cup (50g) chanterelle mushrooms
3/4 cup (50g) champignon mushrooms
1 tablespoon mustard
2 tablespoons balsamic vinegar
3 tablespoons olive oil
sugar, salt, and pepper

Preparation

1. Separate the lettuce leaves, wash, and let dry. Plate the lettuce on four dinner plates.

2. Clean the chanterelles and champignons, slice the champignons. Peel the shallots and dice.

3. Heat oil in a pan and fry the pheasant breast on both sides for about three minutes. Take the pheasant breast out of the pan and keep it warm.

4. Fry the mushrooms in the pan and plate them on top of the lettuce.

5. Brown the shallots in the same pan, then stir in the balsamic vinegar, olive oil, mustard, sugar, salt, and pepper.

6. Cut the pheasant breast into slices and place on the lettuce. Spoon the marinade over it and serve.

7. The lettuce looks especially nice if you decorate it with edible nasturtiums.

Pickled Pheasant with Baked Apples

Ingredients

1 pheasant

For the pickling
1/4 cup (120g) pickling salt
4 cups (1l) water
1 teaspoon juniper berries
2 cloves
1 laurel leaf
1 sprig thyme
3 garlic cloves
1 teaspoon peppercorns

1 cup (1/4l) white wine
3 tablespoons sugar
2 tablespoons clarified butter
3 1/3 cups (200g) wild mushrooms
3 tablespoons butter
1 bunch mixed herbs
1/2 bunch parsley
4 apples
1 small jar cranberries
salt and pepper

Preparation

1. Wash the pheasant, remove feathers if necessary.

2. Put all the pickling ingredients into a pot, cook, and let cool. Put the pheasant in a large bowl and cover with the pickling materials. Place the bowl in the refrigerator covered for at least three days.

3. Take the pheasant out, let it dry well, and stuff the mixed herbs into the pheasant.

4. Grease a fire-resistant baking pan with the clarified butter, put the pheasant into the pan, and bake for about an hour in an oven preheated to 350°F (180°C). Baste the pheasant with its juices regularly.

5. Wash and core the apples and put them in a baking pan with some butter. Fifteen minutes before the pheasant is finished, put them into the oven with the bird.

6. Wash the mushrooms thoroughly. Rinse the parsley and cut it up coarsely. Melt the butter in a pan and fry the mushrooms in it. Season the mushrooms with salt and pepper and sprinkle with parsley.

7. Put the mushrooms on a serving platter, set the pheasant and baked apples on top, and serve.

Tip: This recipe is especially suitable for older pheasants.

Partridge on Balsamic Shallots

Ingredients

4 partridges
3 tablespoons clarified butter
2 cups (500g) shallots
1 1/4 cups (200g) cherry tomatoes
3 tablespoons olive oil
4 tablespoons brown sugar
6 tablespoons balsamic vinegar
3 tablespoons lemon juice
salt and pepper

Preparation

1. Prepare the partridges for roasting, season inside and outside. Put the butter into a frying pan, put the partridges in, and roast for about 45 minutes in an oven preheated to 350°F (180°C). Baste them frequently with its juices.

2. Peel the shallots and halve the bigger ones. Wash the tomatoes and pat them dry.

3. Heat the olive oil in a pan, fry the shallots for 8 minutes. Sprinkle the sugar over them and caramelize them. Pour the balsamic vinegar in, add the lemon juice, and season with salt and pepper. Add the tomatoes to the onions and let sit for about three minutes.

4. Divide the vegetables among four plates and put a partridge on each one.

Partridge with Chestnut Sauce

Ingredients

4 partridges
3 tablespoons frying fat
1 jar chestnuts
3 1/2 tablespoons (50g) butter
1 tablespoon sugar
1 cup (1/4l) vegetable broth
1 glass sweet cream
1 1/3 tablespoons (2cl) brandy
1 sprig thyme
1 package wild rice
salt and pepper

Preparation

1. Prepare the partridges. Season with salt and pepper. Put the partridges in a roasting pan with frying fat and roast in an oven preheated to 350°F (180°C) for about forty-five minutes. Do not forget to baste them.

2. Cook the wild rice as instructed on the package.

3. Drain the chestnuts in a strainer. Melt the butter in a pot and caramelize half the chestnuts in it with the sugar. Pour in the cream and vegetable broth, add the sprig of thyme, and let simmer for about seven minutes. Then take the thyme out of the sauce.

4. Puree the chestnut sauce with an immersion blender and season to taste with the brandy, salt, and pepper. Put the rest of the chestnuts in the sauce and warm it again.

5. Take the partridges out of the oven, divide them, and serve with the sauce and wild rice.

Stewed Partridge with Tarragon

Ingredients

4 partridges
2 tablespoons lemon juice
8 sprigs tarragon
3 1/2 tablespoons (50g) butter
2 shallots
1/2 cup (1/8l) white wine
1 cup (1/4l) chicken broth
1 glass crème fraîche
2 egg whites
2 tablespoons mustard
salt and pepper

Preparation

1. Prepare the partridges for roasting. Rub in the lemon juice, season with salt and pepper, and put a sprig of tarragon in the cavity of each partridge.

2. Peel the shallots and dice. Remove the remaining tarragon leaves from the stems.

3. Melt the butter in a roasting pan and brown the partridges. Add the shallots and the tarragon to the partridges and simmer for a few minutes.

4. Add the chicken broth and white wine and stew covered for about 35 minutes.

5. Take the partridges out of the pot and keep them warm. On low heat, stir the crème fraîche, egg whites, and mustard into the sauce. Beat the sauce with a hand beater, season with salt and pepper, and remove from heat.

6. Plate the partridges and serve with the tarragon sauce.

Quail on Wine Sauerkraut

Ingredients

4 quails
2 tablespoons frying fat
1 tablespoon honey
1 teaspoon paprika powder
5 1/4 cup (750g) sauerkraut
1/2 lb (200g) smoked bacon
2 tablespoons oil

1 onion
2 apples
1 cup (1/4l) white wine
1 laurel leaf
4 juniper berries
1 tablespoon sugar
salt and pepper

Preparation

1. Prepare the quails for roasting and season inside and out with salt and pepper. Put the honey and paprika powder in a bowl and stir with some water.

2. Put the fat and the quails in a roasting pan. Roast for about 25 minutes at 350°F (180°C). Brush often with the honey paprika mixture.

3. Peel the onion and dice, cut the bacon into cubes.

4. Heat the oil in a sauce pan, add the onion and bacon, and brown them. Add the sauerkraut, brown briefly, and pour in the white wine. Sprinkle in the herbs and cook covered for about 15 minutes.

5. Peel the apples and grate them into the sauerkraut with a fine grater. Stir and season to taste with salt and pepper.

6. Take the quails out of the oven and serve on the sauerkraut.

Stuffed Quail Wrapped in Bacon

Ingredients

4 quails
1/2 lb (200g) sliced bacon
1 tablespoon clarified butter

For the stuffing

1 3/4 cup (100g) bread
2 3/4 tablespoons (40g) butter
1 shallot
2 eggs
1/4 lb (100g) chicken liver
1/2 bunch parsley

For the sauce

2 1/8 cups (200g) grapes
1 cup (1/4l) white wine
1 teaspoon cornstarch
1 tablespoon sugar
salt and pepper

Preparation

1. Rinse the parsley, shake it, and pick the leaves from the stems. Peel and dice the shallot. Cut the chicken liver into small pieces and put it in a food processer with the shallot and parsley. Puree the mixture until fine.

2. Cut the bread into cubes, melt the butter in a pan, and fry the bread until golden brown. Mix the bread with the eggs and chicken liver, season with salt and pepper. Let it sit for about 15 minutes

3. Prepare the quails for roasting, season with salt and pepper. Stuff the quails and close the openings with a toothpick. Wrap the quails with the bacon, put into a roasting pan with the butterfat, and roast about forty minutes in an oven preheated to 350°F (180°C).

4. Wash the grapes, halve, and remove larger seeds.

5. Take the quails out of the oven and keep them warm. Deglaze the pan with the white wine. Stir the starch smooth with some water and stir it into the sauce and let it cook. Add the grapes and season to taste with sugar, salt, and pepper.

6. Serve the quails on the grape sauce.

Wild Dove Salad

Ingredients

4 doves
2 tablespoons frying fat
1 glass crème fraîche
1 small chili pepper
1/2 bunch parsley
1/3 cup (50g) pistachio
1 1/3 tablespoons (2cl) brandy
salt and pepper
a variety of salad lettuce
1 shallot
5 tablespoons balsamic vinegar
3 tablespoons olive oil
1 tablespoon sugar

Preparation

1. Prepare the doves for roasting, cut up with shears, and season with salt and pepper. Heat the frying fat in a pan and fry the doves in it. When the doves are finished, take them out of the pan and let them cool. Remove the meat from the bones and cut the larger pieces up.

2. Halve the chili pepper and remove the seeds. Rinse, shake, and pick the parsley leaves. Finely chop the pistachio.

3. Put the dove meat in a blender with the crème fraîche and brandy. Add the chili, parsley, and pistachio and season to taste with salt and pepper. Cover and put it in the refrigerator for about an hour.

4. Detach and wash the lettuce leaves. Make a salad dressing of the finely cut shallot, vinegar, oil, sugar, salt, and pepper.

5. Plate the lettuce, make quenelles of the dove meat with two spoons, and place them on the lettuce. Drizzle with the dressing.

Wild Dove Soup with Mushroom Dumplings

Ingredients

2 doves
6 1/3 cups (1 1/2l) water
1 leek
3 carrots
2 onions
1/2 bunch celery
1 parsley root
1 bunch parsley
1 laurel leaf
4 cloves
1 tablespoon black peppercorns
salt and pepper

For the dumpling

7/8 cups (200ml) milk
1/2 cup (60g) wheat grits
5-6 dried mushrooms (20g)
1 egg
nutmeg
salt

Preparation

1. Put the doves in a tall soup pot with cold water and bring to a boil. After the first boil, reduce the heat and let the doves cook for about an hour. If foam forms on the surface, remove it with a ladle to keep the broth clear.

2. Wash the vegetables, peel or clean them, and cut them into pieces. After 30 minutes, put the prepared vegetables, herbs, and greens into the pot.

3. Take the doves out of the broth, remove the meat from the bones, and cut into strips. Strain the broth into another pot, season with salt and pepper, and add the meat.

4. Put the mushrooms in a bowl and pour hot water over them. When the mushrooms have swollen properly, take them out of the water, press and cut into fine cubes. Boil the milk, add the grits, stir until it separates from the pot, set it aside and let it cool. Stir the mushrooms into the grits and form dumplings using two spoons. Boil in salt water for about five minutes.

5. Take the dumplings out of the water with a spoon, put them into the dove soup, and serve.

Guinea Fowl with Orange Chili Sauce

Ingredients

2 guinea fowls
2 tablespoons frying fat
4 oranges
3/8 cup (100ml) chicken broth
1 glass sweet cream
1 chili pepper
salt and pepper

Preparation

1. Prepare the guinea fowls for roasting and season with salt and pepper, then put them into a roasting pan with the frying fat and roast for about one hour in an oven preheated to 350°F (180°C). Do not forget to baste them.

2. Squeeze two of the oranges, fillet the other two. Halve the chili pepper, remove the seeds, and cut into fine strips.

3. Take the guinea fowls out of the pan and keep them warm.

4. Put the broth, orange juice, and cream into the roasting pan, cook it, and reduce by two thirds. Put the chili strips and orange fillets into the sauce, season with salt and pepper.

5. Carve the guinea fowls and serve with the sauce.

Guinea Fowl with Olive Oregano Stuffing

Ingredients

2 guinea fowls
2 tablespoons frying fat
3 1/3 cups (200g) white bread
1/2 cup (1/8l) milk
1 egg
1/2 cup (50g) green olives
1/2 bunch oregano
2 fennel bulbs
4 tomatoes
2 tablespoons black olives
1 tablespoon sugar
2 tablespoons oil
salt and pepper

Preparation

1. Cut the white bread into cubes, heat the milk, and pour over the bread cubes. Rinse the green olives and cut into rings. Remove the oregano leaves from the stems and cut finely.

2. Add the olives, oregano, and egg to the bread, mix and season with salt and pepper.

3. Prepare the guinea fowls for roasting, season with salt and pepper outside, stuff the bread mixture into the fowls and close the openings with toothpicks.

4. Put the fowls into a roasting pan with frying fat and roast for about one hour in an oven preheated to 350°F (180°C). Do not forget to baste them.

5. Clean the fennel bulbs, wash the tomatoes, and quarter both. Halve the black olives. Heat the oil in a pan, brown the fennel in it, sprinkle in the sugar and let it caramelize.

6. Add the olives and tomatoes, cook briefly, then plate. Halve the guinea fowls, place it on the vegetables, and serve.

Index

We thank the following for their support:

The Food Professionals Köhnen HmbH
Geti Wilba and Gut Adersreuth, cover and pages 13, 17, 21, 37, and 39